Be kind
Be safe
Be human

POEMS BY

OWEN D HILL

Author Bio:

I don't like to write about myself, as I feel it places me in a cage that I must break from. A renegade spirit of sorts. A man of many paths, twists and turns along tributaries less traveled. In some cases, traveling while never leaving my seat. My writing is a simple gaze into the beyond inside my mind, as I deal with the mundane daily rituals, we all face.

Blue collar man of many lives, born a hardscrabble son of a convict. Single mother doing what she could. My southern playground was amongst bikers, ne'er-do-wells, and racists. Salt of the earth people with some ugly truths. Where I learned to navigate my own path to seek truth and understanding.

Born in Florida and taken anywhere food stamps were accepted. And many thanks to Toys for Tots for giving me a glimpse of childhood.

In truth under my skin is a tower of cinders, a black and craggy scar laden soul. My hope is that these books make you think about life or about the lives of others and their struggles.

Thank you for choosing to read my words, it means more than I could ever express. Connect with me @owendhill on social or at www.owendhill.com

Also available on Amazon.com:

CINDERS :poems

Printed in the United States of America

First Printing, 2020

ISBN 9798601537780

www.owendhill.com or @owendhill

Las Vegas, Nevada

10 9 8 7 6 5 4 3 2 1

CONTENTS

INTRODUCTION

To Whom It May Concern:

These poems press on a pain that won't be gentle. There will be words on confusion, love, thoughtfulness, and the reward of learning through life.

They helped me reflect on my experiences that had no easy answers. Sometimes digging up a forgotten hurt needing to be unearthed exposing a nerve not yet dealt with.

I humbly hope you are surprised by words you didn't know you wanted to feel. That somehow, they tap into your own pulse, with startled and stunned emotions that move you, stirring up both the good and bad places. As though I was speaking directly about your experiences but coming from my own.

My reflections will hopefully help you navigate this strange and wondrous life. That if my metaphors have been used wisely you will know we are never truly alone.

So, I leave space in the pages for your imagination to connect to mine.

Be kind, Be Safe, and Be human

Respectfully,

Owen D Hill

EXTENSION LADDER

when we hit bottom

is there a solid point

at which we meet ourselves

the bare boned bane of our existence

a person's soul

to see if they stand up

climbing out into this world

SHEER FALLS

she doesn't think I cry

she'll never understand my pain

my strong stubborn way is not in vain

it's how I've survived my life

my fight for a way

that keeps my path straight

she may never understand

I need my mind with mine

the pain is a peace...and a smile

an ease to the rage

I can't explain other than a why

I search my mind to find it

to bring its ultimate defined demise

or to never find out why...is fine

I may have to wipe my eyes and cry

heart held in hand

telling myself to be light

GAME FATHERS

here is the spring

through summer filled swings

where cold champions fall

based on a game

that reared and molded my frame

as fun to play as it is hard to see

ghosts on a diamond with a ball

a child's eyes wide open

to black barnstormers playing

games of salt and pepper unseen

and the histories of seasons not known

when a monarch fluttered

over a homestead

from coveted virtues of migration

and covered dark in cotton curtains

as men from mobile and good view

met in '42

ESCALATOR MESSAGE

I went down the steps of despair

to take a swim in a pool of lost souls

now I've given the keepers fair

a two-coin cost to pay

the only way is down

at the end was an evil

our last step staring

reflecting in our eyes

where we catch a gaze and say

I have a love...I can't let go

to willingly stand six feet tall

than wallow in this hole

with you and the dead

never speaking truth to power

against this depression and the dread

THE GAME OF GO

black white

and their territory

not so summitry

with all of the ages

and info filled pages

brimming with misery

written a false history

laugh at the laughing

and love the many

micro-visions of a crowd

each as an individual

hidden voices allowed

read aloud

UN-ENTITLED

as darkness increases

my insight focuses

to see with my mind's eye

a created unaugmented honesty

recalling words once wisely given

to my younger self

cultivate expand evolve this

innate vantage seeing the unseen

to make it stick out lucidly

examining in-out-as the environment

to interpret these blueprints

as my mind maps mayhem

mastering this grasp this ability

a virtuoso vision ten steps ahead

looking back in slow-motion hindsight

comprehending connections others cannot see

a cognitive perception mutation metamorphosed

final words of wisdom

you will never be understood...always opposed

approval never needed...give grace to the foes

YOU WANT ME

I feel as though

yet I do not know

my only goal

is to sooth your soul

let mine go

so that our hearts

may flow

REGRET RACE

why can't I see my face

why can't I stay on pace

cause I found love

and lost it too

found it again

and I lost you

FRIENDS AND STRANGERS

I had true love

for just one moment

I seen it coming

I seen it going

you were mine, part of the time

CHEWY TISSUE

to the rest of the country

playmakers join the game

we don't know why

when she smiles

we only sigh

STAY AWAKE

I am an Irishman

that feels as though he's lost

I wander across the rolling hills

and stare across the lochs

I don't believe in the fantasy

that those see'ith in me

for I am merely just a man

trying to live his life in peace

WE ARE DONE

I hate to think
that with a single frown
we turned around
walked away
and stayed that way

I said three words
that shattered her soul
and while she sobbed in hers
I gathered my own

PLANE AS DAY LOOK

open to the sky

as in the darker side

and it rains so much

that I reek with smiles

as chaos comforts me

STRAIGHT JACKET TRACK

first

I am a good liar

second

I am a good storyteller

but the one thing above those

I love everyone

I just won't be

truthful about it

SPRING POLE

dirty little bitch spits

fresh and clean

smiles with a gleam

spite needing weened

doubts laid out in pleasure

as a pushing measure

giving confidence

to fragile little feathers

making comments just to hear their own voice

and ignorant to fact rather than choice

HAPPY HOUR HOME

another year not acknowledged

write me away please

because we don't know him

and should not become him

to get drunk...point a gun

go to prison...all for fun

when running out of luck

gets you run over by a truck

then maybe you'd know him...as a drunk

by the measures and the methods

of skirting responsibilities excused

when being drunk all through life

all the time you use

while never playing sober

the rules of this drinking game

you lose on every occasion when it's over

LIFELETE

talent tricks you

into thinking you have it all

so love this life

in time

working hard helps you when the talent fades

and when the crowd is gone...

your mind can rest in peace

HARD RANKED REALITY

can instincts make you insane

no facts

just feeling

just a question with no answer

only comments in vain

more than a woman or less than a man

peace doesn't mean truth

like love has no proof

faith as always

seems to have a due date master plan

FLATLINE WHISPER

say nothing to me
and I will always find
something to listen to

because there is a someone that has
something to say
even if it isn't you

so speak up loudly
and spill your truth
even if it isn't true

I muzzle no voices
do not try to muzzle mine
just a philosophical convo between me and you

MISMATCHED FORK

life will never end
when they're walking out
simply closing the door
of what didn't work

take a look
at the room around you
four walls, a window
to a world that awaits
needing another look

CERTAINLY NOT THIS TIME

I met a girl named Vicki

who seemed to be quite sticky

along with her general appeal

too nice...too honest...too real

clouded and cluttered we played

she got hers and I got mine

undone surreal...a week later delayed

and she never replied

WRONG DIRECTION

how many corners will I need to turn

until the truth becomes clear

like clean air to breathe

life becoming a breeze

tongues flicker like flame

for sure...but who is to blame

no fault for the burn

wait was that our turn

THIS ALLEY

stand alone

waiting to belong

it comes across

to string us along

from many corners turned in need

until the truth becomes clear

cleaner the air

easier it is to breathe

MEASURED MAN

how does it start

when it cannot begin

to the troubles it brought

and beaten with a heart

bloodletted from the start

carnage as a carnival ride

a man who seeks the truth

just wants a small part

so let these hearts heal pain

and give permission for mine again

TRAVEL PASS

trips never taken

to catch the ray

that fickle fingers touched

the soft sun on that day

chased with brick in hand

gotta catch that bus

to bash and smash a man

singled out in a lane

paid with change

ROCKSTAR RUBE

a poor old soul

having nothing they own

guitar out on loan

with a baby left home

VERY AGGRESSIVE POLE DANCER

little bitch little bitch

run run run

I don't care where you go-go

cause you stole my heart

and left me cold

little bitch

no

no

no

swing round round round on that pole

twist up twist down

I am just a wallet fold

and I know what you're about

COLD BONES

as a look back at your life

it feels as if you have been an adult

since the day you were born

seeing things that are just learned

or known from watching others

old and young all along

the burden ain't yours to bare

life ain't fair...life ain't fair

so breathe a little easier and take care

WILL WE ONLY BE

rain...rain...rain

falling through it all

never having a chance

no choice but to fall

we are as puddles stepped in

a furnished patchwork road

kept fluid with passion and sin

as waterproofed souls out on loan

SPLIT TONGUE

friend in your vocabulary

with a saliva trap bag

that is dripping again

this is the day I leave you

pleading and begging

which is not good for your complexion

what do you really say

to a natural born sun...hun

as real as female

trying so hard

to be the one trick phony

VOODOO SIMPLICITY

lick the wounds clean

soaking them in you

soothe it all away

to stop the spin

with a pained grin

urging to let you know

yearning to give you a peak

that you may take anyway as you go

poked and potioned into submission

forever endlessly on and on

till you fall over in broken down condition

DEEP WHISPERS

her an open ocean

that speaks with whispers

of the deepest darkest fear

telling stories of others lost

and tossed amongst her waves

shells placed against your ear

she speaks about the cost

of echoes from the deep unheard

by ships wrecked along her rocks

and all the chaos caused by us

MADE TO ORDER

left and right of the middle

as minds at the table

move to a new center

finishing your egg roll

don't touch the green stuff

it's way too hot

so pick up the check

and here is a tip

signed the line...shut the fuck up

FILET FEELING

a thought that turns

into a life long dream

how does the mind

let that slip away from grasp

and just mingle into nothing

MUNDANE MENACE

why do I feel as though

I'm being cheated...

by saying nothing at all

it doesn't make a difference

same thing every time

I don't want too

I don't feel like it

but how does that help my esteem

how am I to feel

happy and satisfied in a reply

that is always confronting

my own devout demons

that you don't see

no I don't think you do

and I don't count the doubts

SUB-CONSCIOUS

as fate takes

on two separate paths

is there anymore

energy to continue

with our souls

let's listen

to each other

and walk away

each time

letting the other go

LEAD WINDOW

soaking into the rawness of passion

to probe beneath

an elaborately thick moment

think above your favorite stream

smear your head

over a forest of human lives

sky bitter and smooth

but always behind

you give before giving

compassion and integrity

a false sense of progress

performed to please well

PROPOSAL

smooth a bitter woman's storm

so she can play

her languid picture

in a lathered juice

of an enormous diamond

heaving on piles of empty love

to a place of deliriousness

the succulent liquor

in a plot to kill a man

screaming commitment alone

ticking down days

one by one by one

BIG IF

if

misery

loves

company

does

that

mean

happiness

loves

being

an

individual

TOILET TALKING MONARCH

curly auburn hair

freckled and fair

talking into the big white phone

listen to your voice echo

round and round its goes

anything of worthy value flushed

with chunked up hair unbrushed

down through your self-made crown

mounted upside down

a perfect fitting porcelain throne

made all your own

FUTURE

a lost soul cries

making the mind fly

as fellow people leave them

to weep alone

in a no stakes sadness

no path home

me, myself, and I

NOT IN SERVICE

when I asked

you were so quick

to shake your head

stopping at every moment

letting me in your mind

apiece to know you more

all I want to like I reject

is this really for me to solve

I don't know

when you always ask for a hug

your mouth hangs wide open

like being surprised why I say no

I guess I push you so far outside

that your reality really needs a sign

with directions you are too broken to see

NOT MY IDEA / NOTHING POEM

sitting back where no people go

behind the signs

what is in those people's heads

does it ever really matter

people see only what they like

people always want what others have

if we reached into everyone

as if we knew all people's thoughts

at once

would people stop at what moved them

or would they cave

under the weight of all the emptiness

people wouldn't like to know my thoughts

1.
at the heart of every person is a
sound something so deep that it
resonates like a pressure in your
chest it is this feeling that the
individual seeks to make heard not
merely to emphasize the chases
clinches climaxes or to smooth over
the indecencies of life and it's
shaky breakups but to give voice to
an inner life it's soul if such a
thing can be said of love

2.
what we evoke with the piping voices
of our feelings we project its
images with a grace and tragedy no
words could ever express as we begin
working on love and life with its
savage nature a dark and bloody
heart a love both overwhelming and
destructive the struggles of
personalities for their right of
passion

3.

the harmonies of the ancestral place
from which the past relationships
have come and the melodies of the
obscured future places which will
represent our future relationships
and the ties that bind them all that
can be said to distill cascading
lofty conversations in a single life
is all at once brooding and lush
redolent of love and loss equally
touching the secret place of awe
inside us all everywhere at once in
time for generations moments this is
a consequence usually experienced
only once before during our birth

AGED BRANDY

newborn to the peddler's world

my curiosity keeps my eyes stuck

wide open and dried out

when I blink I notice it

auburn in color and a corkscrew curl

it has the smell of something permanent

with a mild taste of poison

the one of my choice of course

it's bitter with an imaginably sweet taste

and all the more droplets each hour

my glutton will kill each second

and I should have gone thirsty

ONE SUPER BIG GULP

our two bashful hearts

our sweaty palms

stick across our

blank pages

LOST

kiss me softly

hold me slowly

leave me quickly

love me forever

TURNS TO REAL

we were busy pointing fingers

and busy placing the blame

instead of realizing the heart we'd lose

at the end of this little game

IMAGINE IT YOURSELF

I set a rose petal bath for you
waiting for you to arrive
to lead you to a crucial cleanse
dismantling your clothing
exposing your skin

you slide into the water
its warmth tickling your pores
and I sponge your body
to take this day away

when you stand from the water
the petals stick to your skin
and I place a kiss
where each petal lay

LAST NIGHT

she was in a cold sweat

huddled in a ball

prying her limbs free

I whisper to her as she woke

a glaring look upon her face

as she sat there staring into my eyes

my arms clinched around her body

sleep now...its ok

go back to sleep

you'll have sweet dreams

COMING BACK TO LIFE

I can taste you on my lips

smell you in my clothes

touch you in my dreams

and feel you in my tears

FOREVER LIFE A DAY

would I miss you on a lonely day

when life makes me feel unworthy

where you could hold me as I cry

would I miss you on a lovely day

when existence is all I'd ever ask for

where you could live it all with me

would I miss you on the longest day

when my life is at its closure

where we could say our last goodbyes

in truth I'd only miss you

if we never had our time

we are intertwined...this is our life

INNERLIFE LESSON

when I had to ask for love

I never knew I had it

but now I do not ask

I know I did

and lost it

twice

CROSS WORLDS APART

let me see your eyes

let me feel your skin

let me in your heart

let our life begin

again and again and again

TWENTY-FOUR SEVEN

if I could hold your body

close to me tonight

if I could speak to you softly

there will be no more fright

CUPID TYPE TAILGATING

please do not cry tonight

I still love you

yet I feel it slipping away

my mind does not believe your shame

but my heart does

and inside this

it never felt so wrong

as it falls apart and crushes me

what should I do

no choice but sleep for tonight

now it is gone

STREET WALKING MAID

my room is a mess
I don't want to clean it
I'd rather screen my laziness
with no bed folds who would care

it's time for work
to be up all night
consequences with being adult
fetished posts in dreamy streams

my POV for all to see
contentually bottomed in my control
as with my entertainment
my loyal following will be on soon

my room is a mess
and so is everything else
but at least I get to smile
every time they venmo me

STILL HAVE MY MONEY

when they arrived

I was already hidden

they didn't find me

but that dumpster stunk

ME AND YOUR GIRL

you were touching me

in the next room

your heart beating

into my chest

its persistence leaving

an untellable imprint

through this rollercoaster

ride of silence

where we will cum soon

to a complete stop

and he wouldn't like it

if he knew

you did not only want to talk

POUNDING

it might as well

be you

with your crying little heart

your lowered

self-esteem

and your over exceeding

fat consciousness

and you

already so well anorexily built

yet you

and the rest of the world

are now

in the worshipping of the bean pole

your ribs as wrapping

while starving

head as a bow

industry pushed package size zero

approval in the hands of an editor

glossy covers for gluttons

but you can never eat

PREDATOR MEETS PREY

please feed my little head

I don't want to hide

behind my white picket fence

anymore

I would like to see that side

your side or at least hear about it

anyway

I have been pampered

solid silver spoon fed, I will do

anything

it is not my fault

I didn't ask to be

spoiled

I promise you

I will do whatever you say

I will be

loyal

I want to feel and see

the dirty place you call home

its gritty

soil

please feed my little head

tell me teach me make me see

the other side

BLOWN BULB

past pictures
a boy left alone
an element of silence
leaves him vulnerable

the churning stomach
a preaching child
his envisioned outcome
with that woman

his lonely childhood
dipped into the future
with an irrevocable past
as a logical flipbook

deprived of tender grace

engraved with negligence

the unspoken mind over weighted

and then shut off

presenting pictures

an unrestrained child

heart hunger pangs on

malnourished and malignant

future pictures

energies now turned up

and she wonders why

the switch doesn't work

FEMALE EAU DE TOILETTE

still smell her

she was here in my arms

in my room

still smell her

her hair, she left some hair

in my bed

still smell her

her smell it's on my sweater

on my sheets, on my pillow

oh my pillow, this is where

her head laid while she slept

next to me, in my bed

in my arms she laid

still smell her

her shirt, she left her shirt

and it smells like her too

now a need to return her shirt

to smell her again

that sweet intoxicating scent of her

DELTA

one person

making you laugh

making you cry

making you hurt

that ache

in the center

of your chest

in the bottom

of your throat

love is not mercy

terrifically tremendous

tediously terrible

taxing tenderly

throughout time

TEN WAYS TO SUCCEED WITH THEM

1. be on time

2. be prepared

3. bring a pen or pencil   .

4. come when asked...always alone

5. think about me only...all the time

6. friends and family come second

7. your job and extra-curricular activities
   come second to me

8. must be personal chauffeur whenever
   transportation is needed

9. say "ok, I will" in the response to anything
   and everything asked of you

10. treat me the way "I" want to be treated

(contractually obligated: all the following is
      required for this relationship)

strange list not followed

WHEN COUNTING NEVER COUNTS DOWN

69 times enjoyed it

68 songs played it

67 fantasies played with

66 g-spots tickled in

65 places done it

64 flavors remembered

63 juices that touched it

62 stages reached it

61 colors that have seen it

60 hours felt it

59 smells that came from it

58 times couldn't continue

57 ways liked it shaved

56 reasons you get it

strange list well followed

SUPER WHITE MARY JANE

blondie blondie

with the dark roots

I can see

there is a glimmer

from your shiny boots

as you say

hey baby...smile at me

while you lick your finger

like it was cookies and cream

and then talked of a double team

stalking me down the street

my my what a shame

your life you've wasted

mary jane

platform pumps high

streetwise past prime

face fully pasted

fiscally tricky trade

WHY

I ask everything

whether it makes sense

to you or not

is it still as good as the next

a repetitive question?

are questions for your own knowledge

the things you know the answer too

but just won't admit

LOW-VAULTED PAST

I stood on that park bench

waiting for you

down that cold trail

you never coming

I guess you

decided not to see me

anymore

but I stayed...

and waited anyway

flowers in hand frozen stiff

sitting there...

shivering in the damp cold

I sat and watched

my breath makes lonely shapes

AUTOTUNED TAMBOURINE MAN

floating high above your head

he swoops down

to run in...and sit

to talk to your dreams

he likes to make it all slip away

yeah that little man

with black hair and curly beard

who swears he would die with you

or make it all go away

for just a little while

he says hope you're feeling better

read from a little florist letter

stuck in with a plastic pitchfork

out of your acid rained plant

HILUM

a tiny little mark

that had its purpose meant

at the beginning of the game

old as time is nature's intent

unfinished tunnel leading to your back

your siblings detached all the same

always on the opposite side of the crack

no one ever remembers the snip

as greens are unaware in sprout

not a pocket but still with lint

eye catching when some stick out

magical yet simple

important with no clout

we only notice the dimple

left as a clever little cleft

HEART IS SUICIDAL BLISS

to look at beauty

the way I see it

is when she touches your hand

holds you in her heart

stares into your eyes

turns around and walks away

to leave you wondering

where she will lead you next

LITTLE PLASTIC TOYS

little plastic toys
you made for me on my birthday
they were cute and cheap
but I love them all the same

well maybe not

silly you can yell at me
beat me...and smack me in the head

your little third world hand always stung
like a cat-of-nine-tails
wrapped in skeletons from a closet

but you know I started to think tonight
I hate those little plastic toys you make
grown in fields from political wars
spoils of hacks and hawks galore
in two-button blue jackets sending boys to die
but never their own privileged child

SUNSHINE

when difficult days

are nearly done

that warm feeling felt

is from only one

of noted beams like songs on air

she emblazones everywhere

a glow for the world and I

as we share relevance in the sky

its lovely in the rising light

every morning and after each night

on the other side

while etched in the blue

she adorns you

ARE YOU CLINICALLY TESTED

you said to call at two

and I called you

you said to meet you

and I met you

you said to stay with you

and I refused you

you said you wanted too

and I ignored you

you said I confused you

and I explained to you

you said I want to

and I questioned you

you said it's for you

and I chose not too

you said I want to...for you

and then I left you

UP ALL NIGHT THAT NIGHT

because I saw something in her eyes

I asked her softly what was wrong

and she ignored me

at first

then she said, "I'll tell you later."

I asked why again

and again

because the why disturbed me

she said she couldn't tell me now

she said

"don't worry"

it is not important

but I wanted to know

then she said

with a whisper in her mind

roll over...please

LEGACY

seventy-eight years an old man

working in a field of clouds

his dewy plow sifting

the crumb cake soil

as he speaks to his oxen

drilling through a field of fog

his mind flickers into his life

reminiscence the wife he teamed with

their fertility unplundered by god

eight children sporadically in eleven years

their prosperity sounding from within

a house of young pitter patter

the eighth child the last

along with the touch of one-another

they bedding next to an unfilled imprint

in straw filled seed sacks

the bed of ending generation

how she longed for his wood roughened hands

the slightly painful scuff

of his unshaven whiskers

his gnarled knuckles without tender care

the wounds mending themselves

scars the reminder their lacks a second half

their relinquished young patters

for the legacy that is to live

apart in touch deprived of warmth

tied by the grand new patters

for the future children and theirs to come

sacrifices unwanted yet somehow forced

legacy that is to live within their offspring

is the soil that is to be passed along

each guarding the final home

beneath their own stones

he and his wife touching again

SKATEBOARD IRONY

he felt like killing himself today

would he be able to do it

no...he never could

I think he only talks of it

that way he is not afraid

to die

but this is no time to fall down

because then he'll never get up and ride

6 years later, he was gone

when he was happy in life

SUBSTANCE ANCHOR

this petty life I lead

strings me along

and makes me bleed

tying me down

gleefully in its roots

gripping down on my boots

I don't know why I traded you away

for a common red nose clown

anchored in needle it shoots

celebrity heroin his big red shoes

as red pillows in like your hate

their colors run streaming

bright... true... straight...

flying crooked on a trip

CROSSWORD WALK

little lady sassafras

walking through my life

flaunting all that sass

stomped right in

stomped right out

now a memory of the past

intelligent man talks

a wise man walks

but many men

pay to play

for your glory

MY THOUGHTS THEN THE DOG TYPED IN

```
petty people play as puppets

praying for possessions

in exorbitant ways these days

driven by drastic errors

as social media sucks up time

mnjjjjjjjj

p=-[oi;;;;;;;;;;;;;;;;;;

;;;;;;;;;;;;;;;

;;;;;;;;;;;'juipl vgg
```

TRANSLATOR

hecklers call out

and they tug at my face

while the bleeding hearts pump

although it is in a waste

of worded clout

SLOWLY WALKED

I can't run from this

I can hide my eyes

as leachy love lessons

prey upon my cries

in an aisle of exile

with unthrown rice

birdseed all handed out

to save the future

of a wild bird that flies

fleeing unlike me

SECRETS SHOPPING

people coming people going

never finding out

I sit back

where no one knows

what goes on in my head

watching and keeping track

it doesn't matter what I think

or if I see what I like shown

customer service rendered and polite

means maybe I'll be back

grading as I go

sometimes I want what I see

if they knew what I really know

it'd change it all completely

but come push to shove we'd all have a go

SPEEDBALL

am I the last gesture

from a turn that came smashing straight

when you flew past me

through the window

landing next to a tree

the other side of the road

your head cut up and bleeding

lip busted split badly

looking as though you were dreaming

but only dead

slumping from the gravity

BRITISH TOOTHPICK

tis the fain lady

I seek amidst the night

too dip thine own eyes

into her tender heart

like tapas spread amongst a group

shared taste

shared smile

shared air

shared wilds

ENTROPICAL ILLUSIONS

our life was lost

when we hit the floor

there is a high-end cost

for what's in store

spent too much time in pain

crawling on hands and knees

begging and screaming in vain

but we don't walk away

neither of us choose to leave

as if nothing changed along the way

we are cowards that won't grieve

two tortured souls in a living grave

because of our life

seems like we lied

unworthy from within

uncomfortable in our skin

you wrecked me

FERRIS WHEEL BUCKET LIST

tilt-a-whirl girl

and me

riding as bucket seat debris

in silence all the way round

trying to not draw a crowd

locked in

strapped

for the ride

shoot your shot

in a torn magnum ticket

full of pride

organic seeds for any vegan

or so she said

with an endless dent

on this mind bent carnival ride

little white baggy of donation

left for the next ticket toting patron

YOU WILL BECAUSE YOU CAN

who can tell me no

who can tell me to go

who will stand their ground

who will fuck around

who can bring it forward

who can bring it back

who will fuck it up

why spend your time on

thinking negative of others?

people's eyes see the shell

the barriers of the virgin lie

the screen guarding the mind

and emotions completely corrupt

worlds offered so bluntly but false

manufactured silver plattered material

awards as way of life possessed

by even the most moral

people are a junction of giving

time with yourself in mind

melding these ways of life together

attention means only one thing

you like that pretty saliva tray

engraved with your account name

and teething rings from tiffany's

miserly craving your view count

LIFEBOAT WORMHOLES

riddles are everywhere

the strands of life themselves

there is no one answer

for riddles of the mind

the most astute of us

must create a tidal wave of whit

to tell us how we are feeling...

the questions

found puzzling and then left alone

as if it were never heard of

all the brilliant ones giving up

because trying is just too hard

given the space and time

in an ignorant destitution

TWO OF FOUR WALLS

today

we were honest again

true to our feelings

as we spoke out loud

into each other's ears

and stared into each other's eyes

with a little love and a little hate

hearing her as she heard me

at peace or at least at truth

THE OTHER TWO WALLS

today

we laughed and cried and bonded again

wrapped up in our thoughts

as we laughed and chuckled

into each other's arms

and savored each other's warmth

with a little smile and a little frown

I thought and she thought too

we were honest again in peace

though we share the same city

and we feel the same sun

when your final winter comes

I will be the last one...to know you

...THAT you

the one who did not choose what was done

whose brother and father are to blame

as mother's watchful eye looking away

doing nothing but obscuring love causing pain

I had to leave

or I would have killed them both

if they touched our future child

our baby would not carry their shame

or your denial

as you keep abusers close

see I was committed in ways you never knew

in my moral marrow I couldn't marry you...

yet I hope you find freedom from that darkness

INFLUENCER

nothing of deep thoughts

or things to think about

on a giant wheel for hopeful fortune

all just dreams that spin round and round

gaining hunger each day

each follower

wishing for a little more of the life

with a filter that is not promised

but thought is wanted

quotes by great people

posted by fake people

as reality is wasted in clicks

scrolling on

VALENTINE PRINCIPLES

she loves me

she loves me not

this is the first day

that I forgot

my love

hello...hello...

did you hang up?

is that another man there?

an all for nothing love

a stale chocolate heart

and flowers to go

DRUNK SHOW OF POWER

a woman says

buy the bottle

let us go

into that alley

over there where

she takes his jaw

forcing her tongue

down his throat

a man doing what

any man would do

squeezing her body

into his excitement

against the wall

she then places

that full bottle

under her arm

kisses his cheek

and walks away

ABORTED CLAUSE

you'll get hooked

you'll get drugged

she'll be your essence

she'll be your blood

if only that choice was yours

it was

ONE HOT MINUTE

clink-clink of the saucer

my nervous hand trembles

at the fingertips

as I fill my mouth

with piping hot coffee

and spiced crumb cake

this long drawn out hour

clatter...clatter...chit...and chatter

to discuss me in nine months

or if I will be gone

is to be an old topic

at least until the birth

in this wonderful year of 1956

JUST TALKING DISCIPLINE

between my fingers and my thumb
a sweaty palm sits clinched
like a bear trap unsprung

under my breath a thought boils
in repliance to a back hand
turned on a child
while his mother is talking
I stare her down...in angst

still a suffocating lump in my chest
says to stay away and turn around
don't react leave it alone
but she stoops so low
while hitting high in voice
as though she has no choice

an assailant in a lavender dress
make-up done hair did to embellish

fresh from the beauty shop

that crack of flesh on flesh

little boy's eyes don't even balk

this conflict is a common threat

her taloned hand clamped

on the neck of her child

eagles' claws caught its prey

her deed not completely done

rooted talons dug in and bleeding

scattering any new thoughts

or comments that she is wrong

her only loving the thrill

of being an overseer more than a mom

as abuse is layered and laid out

as though it was clean linens

a con woman's normal conversation

an inevitable joke twisted and turned
she belittles at any cost
then swallows it as she smiles
as acting in perfection to an audience

nicking and slicing vigorously
never ending little comments
over nothing of importance
but hurting with every word
her satisfaction of superiority talking

cold chills chafe down my spine
imagining living through his thoughts
the questions swirling around my head
that I have no armor to defeat her
the dread of a motherly evil heart
following a suit in no business of mine

911 I would like to report a crime

The final pages are Existential Abstractions... these are some simple words to describe an essence or give small fragments of each poem.

Kernels of an image if you are lost by my intention...or sometimes to enable an abstract place to get lost in thought.

Completely your own interpretation though, these riddles and rambles have no sacred answers.

Ultimately if you find yourself going back time and time again to seek an understanding or find the usefulness in a metaphor, then maybe I've done a good job.

It's all about seeking connection...or creating them. Thank You.

EXISTENTIAL ABSTRACTIONS

13 extension ladder || soul / existence / fight

14 sheer falls || pain / compassion / recognition / self

15 game fathers || understanding / family / negro league baseball

16 escalator message || death / self-love / depression

17 the game of go || oppression / slavery / falsehood

18 un-entitled || thought / mind / perspective / self / autism

19 you want me || love / goals / easiness

20 regret race || love / loss

21 friends and strangers || love / loss / time

22 chewy tissue || smile / idea / game / miscommunication

23 stay awake || travel / lost / in peace / humility

24 we are done || relationships / love / break up

25 plane as day look || ideas / thought experiment on dimensions

26 straight jacket track || truth / lies / self-indulgence

27 spring pole || talking points / marxism / marginalization

28 happy hour home || family / addiction / excuses

29 lifelete || wasted talent / life / time

30 hard ranked reality || time / faith / sanity

31 flatline whisper || speech / communication / relationships

32 mismatched fork || love / loss / relationships / dating

33 certainly not this time || sex / lust / disappear / dating

34 wrong direction || future / travel / direction / shit talking

35 this alley || mistakes / climate / silence

36 measured man || heart / healing / self-given permission

37 travel pass || chase / owing / pain

38 rockstar rube || dead dreams / lost / out-of-time

39 very aggressive pole dancer || sex worker / money / begging

40 cold bones || age / life / lessons

41 will we only be || nature / no choice / temporary life

42 split tongue || friend / love / leaving

43 voodoo simplicity || relationships / sex / games

44 deep whispers || nature / speaking / climate change

45 made to order || movement / conservative climate talking point

46 filet feeling || dream / past / change

47 mundane menace || sex / relationships / doubts

48 sub-conscious || listening / life / path

49 lead window || media / regression / false progress

50 proposal || woman / death / anger

51 big if || misery / happiness

52 toilet talking monarch || addiction / toilet / puke

53 future || soul / mind / lost

54 not in service || unhealthy relationship / mental illness / giving

55 not my idea/nothing poem || watching / thought

56 unnamed numbers || heart / healing / birth / string of consciousness

58 aged brandy || sex / dating an older woman / relationship

59 one super big gulp || young love / sex / life / convenient

60 lost || love / loss / forever

61 turns to real || loss / blame / pointing

62 imagine it yourself || sensual / affection / touch / release

63 last night || ptsd / rape victim / support / giving / sleep

64 coming back to life || emotion / warmth / lost

65 forever life a day || death / grief / life / longing

66 innerlife lesson || love / loss / choice

67 cross worlds apart || love / time / reincarnation / soulmate

68 twenty-four seven || affection / safety / nightmares / ptsd / rape victim

69 cupid type tailgating || ending / no closure / love

70 street walking maid || sex worker / Instagram / tinder date

71 still have my money || mugging / seedy city / hiding

72 me and your girl || sex / betray / cheating / female sexuality

73 pounding || esteem / vanity / model industry

74 predator meets prey || molestation / pining / predator

76 blown bulb || upbringing / mother / negligence / ignored

78 female eau de toilet || smell / warmth / love

79 delta || love / connection / emotion

80 ten ways to succeed with them || demanding / nonsense / relationship

81 counting never counts down || experienced / nonsense / relationship

82 super white mary jane || sex work / temptation / ancient trade

83 why || questioning / thought / group think

84 low-vaulted past || waiting / lonely / love

85 autotuned tambourine man || drugs / acid / hallucination

86 hilum || nature / connection / bellybutton

87 heart is suicidal bliss || beauty / leading / heart

88 little plastic toys || military industrial complex / politics / politicians

89 sunshine || sun / earth / sunshine

90 are you clinically tested || bipolar / relationship / miscommunications

91 up all night that night || sleep / angry / silence

92 legacy || family / life / ancestors / love

94 skateboard irony || suicide / friends / depression

95 substance anchor || loss / hate / addiction / drugs

96 crossword talk || sex worker / lust / attitude

97 my thoughts then the dog typed in || petty / people / play / social media

98 translator || heckler / bleeding / waste

99 slowly walked || prey / love / marriage

100 secrets shopping || watching / thought / robbery / dating

101 speedball || crash / death / dreaming

102 british toothpick || heart / shared experience / accents

103 entropical illusions || anger / love loss / end of days / apocalyptic

104 ferris wheel bucket list || sex / white trash / young love / carnival

105 you will because you can || negativity / thinking / time

106 first course impressions || social media / fraud / self-centered / ego

107 lifeboat wormholes || questions / depression / ignorance is bliss

108 two of four walls || living together / relationship talk / love / truth

109 the other two walls || living together / truth / in peace

110 she lies to hide a shame not her own || lies / incest / molestation

111 influencer || spent youth / waste / time / social media

112 valentine principles || lost its meaning / empty / commercial

113 drunk show of power || mystery / alcohol / lustful confusion

114 aborted clause || abortion / prochoice / death

115 one hot minute || abortion / shotgun wedding / leaving

116 just talking discipline || child abuse / love / hate / lies

Printed in Great Britain
by Amazon